WHEN MY SOUL WAS UNDONE

By: Marla Mason

Marla Mason

TABLE OF CONTENTS

This book is for my children,

Nyomi and Kai

Know that you have been my best decisions. You

are the better pieces of me.

I love you with all my heart.

To my mother, your strength resides in me always. This is for you too.

Special Thanks To:

Erica and Taylencia

I don't know where this book would be without either of

your constant love and support. Thank

you. Always.

DEAR LORD,

I've Been Running

Caged Bird

I didn't write for seven years
I kept my thoughts isolated
My emotions caged
I held in toxins
That spewed out of my pores
I was a womb of
Contradictions and metaphors
Holding onto baggage
That was never mine to hold
I didn't write
So I didn't speak
About the pain I was living
But even caged birds learn how to sing

Words

Words dance on my tongue
Like loose drops of water
Falling from leaves
They are the hidden words I swallowed
When he pinned me down
Spreading my knees
He cursed my every movement
I was the victim of his witch hunt
I crawled out of my skin
And tried to pretend
My body was no longer Hell
But dammit, I was wrong
I kept those words
Buried in mental caskets
I fasted and prayed
With anger and rage
For my pain to fade
Only to find that those words I swallowed
Never died
They choked me
Took whole breaths from my being
Left me clinching baby sized stitches
With hip-to-hip scars
Words like water droplets
Danced out my mouth into
My pool of tears
Like mixing blood and water
These blurred lines fade
Between peace and insanity
These hidden words
Are brazenly terrifying

Mending

Being raped
Before knowing love
Is the hardest part of me
To mend

The pain still oozes
From the air that escapes my lungs

Why did I experience
Hell
When I was living
A dream

Being raped
Still frightens me

And it's only
The words
I'm viewing

Ruined memories
Shattered pieces

When collected and tallied
Are live images I'm still escaping

Being raped

Before falling in love

Changes. Everything.

No different

When did my silence
Become permission
For your hands to roam?
For your lips to touch?

When did my whispered no's
Become the background sounds'
Of your ego?

When did we get here?

Weak interpretations of consent
I thought you were better
Than those past men

Cried

I cried the night he raped me

Waited for my soul to reconnect
With my body
Waited for my mind
To deny what I knew happened
Waited for the shame
To climb on top of me
Like he did

I screamed the night
He held me down
Like the belly of my being
Had come undone

I felt the softest parts of me
Die
Resurrect
And come back
Changed

I cried the night he raped me
Because
I knew I lost a piece of me
I'd never get back again

Searching

How can I give love
When it was robbed from me?

I've been watching
Fairy tales
And placing bets
On a fantasy
That real love still exists'

How do I get justice
When all my love has been pain?

How do I heal these
Rusty, withered, broken
Pieces of me?

Danger

I anticipate they'll stay
When they only planned
To enjoy moments
Of my love

Fooled into intimacy

I'm a danger to my own heart

Murderer

I murdered the sounds of my children
Before they had a chance
To breathe

Their blood mixed
In my water
Life snatched
From their souls

I aborted

Sins
Bathed in shame
I murdered the muttered
Sounds of my voice
Breaking my own heart
Expecting to find love

But this pain is greater
Then any love I've felt

Where's the healing
If I'm still grieving

Bloody Hands

For the longest time
I hated my cycle

It reminded me of the days
I spent releasing his seed
From my body

Clotted layers of pain
And fear
Mark the memory of the children
I never named

Visions muted under distress

For the longest time
I felt disconnected
From myself

Deep down I hated these secrets
I kept sealed between my legs
And across my heart
Speaking only in silence
While bowing to pray
For my sins to be cleansed

But these painful memories
Never wash away

I used to hate my cycle
It reminded me that their blood
Was still on my hands

War Zone

The basin of my heart
Is filled with the old hopes and promises from ex lovers

It feels like I'll never be rid of their residue
Their webs were sticky and dense

Heavy and tiresome were the ways
They handled me

I want heaven again

Like childhood days
When my heart was light as air
And the world hadn't consumed me

If only I could clean these gaping wounds
These trenches in my heart

DEAR EMPTINESS,

I Struggle to Carry The Weight Of You

Empath

I fell in love with your melancholy.
It was the one thing that consumed my shadows.

I found myself drowning in sorrows.
While trying to save us both.

I felt trapped

Like those dreams you have.
Where there's no sound.
But you're screaming at the top of your lungs.
Looking for the light.
Under the door.
Or anywhere.

I fell
In your love.
It was murky.
With damp air.

I knew the rivers in your eyes resembled the Mississippi.
They were still on the surface yet
Turbulent underneath.

But somehow I chose.
To try mending you.

Pass Over

Her eyes danced like shadows
From chandeliers
She couldn't face me without tears
Running

She was afraid of goodbyes

No one ever stayed long enough
For her to know what love was
She was always the one right before
The one
Always left for the next
Never sheltered from the rest
She was the test

She wanted love
A one way ticket
With no date of return
She was a keeper of
Their love

Who was created to keep her?

Heart Potion

I still remember your heartbeat
It would dance in the palm of my hand
Whose sonnets are you feeding now?
Oh the power you render freely
Stolen hearts kept under lock and key.

Incomplete

Where do you go
When the whole world
Is nowhere to be found?

Days pass in moments
And everyday
Is a reminder
That you are not here

Where do you run
When the chase ends?

What happens when love
Calls your name
And you don't respond
In time?

I guess we all
Find that love and time
Are related
They wait for no one

Different

I called you last night
My heart left a voicemail

Your ego declined
To return my call

I know you've heard the messages

My heart echoed apologies
Like tattooed names
On fresh skin

You're different now
Did my call come too late

I called you last night
While you were calling
A different name

Home

The music we played on those late nights
Still echo in my mind
Your smile still lingers
Like framed photographs
In the gallery of my heart
These memories don't feel like memories at all
I'm still waiting for your call
Waiting for you to tell me
That you want to come home

Walls

We spoke that night

And I watched you hide behind smiles
And words you seldom use

You were attempting to protect your heart

I was becoming
The enemy

A stranger from your past

How does love
Twist and turn
Into the distance
I just want you back

Distance

The distance leaves us in limbo
It's easier to walk away
Than together
When the distance between us
Is hundreds of miles long

Broken Heart

Sometimes
There are no words
For what you feel

Sometimes
Being still
Is the only way
To numb the pain

Mourning

I thought about you today
The sound of your voice
The touch of your fingertips
Your softly spoken words
It's amazing how these things only live in memories
Only survive through my thoughts
If only I could turn back time
Just to replay moments
Like these
Maybe moving on would be easier
Maybe my heart would break slower
Allowing room to heal
Unlike now
These days I replay your smile
In our bed
As light pierces through our white shutter blinds
And it hits me
You're gone
And all these memories
Are service to our memorial
I'll cry flowers everyday
At our wake
Until I no longer see your smile
In my bed

Connected

I felt you today
Your tears fell
Hundreds of miles away
And stained the shoulders of my shirt
I could hear
Your heart calling for me
I wanted to call you
But these wounds still need healing
I miss loving you
You were the best part of our story

Recalling

My heart breaks everytime I hear your name
We were something magical
Yet destructive all at once
I loved you in ways I never knew existed
Held you in ways my father holds my mother
I was yours
I was yours
And all I ever wanted was you

My Last

I would have given you my last
Breath
Song
Tear
Love story
I would have given you my all
But that was then
Now
I find myself
Reminiscing
Old times
Smiles
Love
And progression.
I would have given you my everything
But we didn't last.

Marla Mason

Always

I held back tears today
Thinking of you
Missing the pieces of you that made me smile
I swear the tears in my eyes became heavy
Like frozen paint cans during winter
I've been feeling my heart beat slower
It's colder here now that you're gone
The trees are bare
The air is stale
All I want is spring again
Always wishing you the best.

The Old

Im learning pieces of me
I remember mending
Somehow these scars
Have me visually blending
Healed from healing
I want to be in a better place
Somewhere between her heart and her hands
But my soul is weary
Tired of feeling incomplete
I wish I knew the beauty she sees
Im learning pieces I reconstructed
Long ago
I guess it's time for me
To learn how grow out of the old
I want to be in love again
I want to mend these tortured pieces
The ones hidden from me
In places I've neglected
Resorting to melancholy
And weeping
I want to be a blossom
Of flowers in the spring
I'm guessing our processes
Are similar
Growing out of one's old
Self
Blooming into
New beauty
I want be a
Blossom in Spring

The Ending

Today my heart is disconnected
My thoughts silenced
Today begins the grieving
Of you and I
Present hopes
Turned into past lies
I was ready for you
You were not ready for the change
Necessary for us to thrive
Saying goodbye
Is always the hardest part
Here's to the many ways
Love dies

DEAR LOVE,

When Are You Going To Stay?

Marla Mason

Deep Cuts

How do I love you
When you use
The edges of your
Broken heart
To console me?

The Real You

Please,
Tell me all the lies
You told your mother
Tell me all the lies
You told your father
Tell me all the lies
You tell yourself
Tell me all your lies

I want to recognize your truth
Long before your lies present a perfect picture of who you ought
to be

I want your failures and mistakes on the table
I want you raw and uncanny
I want your ugly truth
I want the real you in ways that leave you open
I want the pieces you hide
In fear of being candid with your love
Show me the real you

Marla Mason

Drowning in Your Love

I ran into the pool of your love
Expecting ecstacy

Not realizing I'd drown

Your love drowned me
And I needed saving

On My Mind

You have become my every thought
Just as you planned
Now my waking moments are infiltrated
With notions of loving you
How could I ever be sane again

Fragile

I find myself falling in love
Quickly
Romancing the honeymoon phase
Neglecting all the red flags and warning signs
I dive into the river of your promises
Not realizing
Falling quickly
Ends things abruptly
Leaving one's heart
Rigid
Uneven in texture and thought
Falling too quickly is my
Specialty
Be careful with my frail heart

Regret

I waited
When you chose her
I stood by
When you used me
I waited
For you to choose me
I waited
For you
And abandoned the life I should of lived

Oxygen

It's as if you take
The oxygen out of the room
I want to be angry
But the very breath that fuels me
Has already been consumed

My unsettled emotions leave me speechless
I am both angry and intrigued in the wake of your distraction
Missing you has left variance in my demeanor
Now, I'm hoping I could catch my breath
Long enough to enjoy you

Stay

She asked me to stay a while
Complex problems need solving
I found myself crowded
In her space
She wanted me to stay
But never intended
On making room for
This chaos called my heart

Ache

My heart broke too
When I first realized
Someone else would be loving you

Remnants

I left pieces of me
In the pockets of your soul

Tequila Shots

I ordered my heartache
Heavy handed
Neat
Now I find myself
Chasing
Memories
Too sour to stomach

Images

What am I to do
When your smile
Still lingers in my photo album?

Who do I call to tell you
How much I miss you?

How your eyes have been on my mind

How do I walk away
When all I've ever wanted was for you to stay?

What am I to do
When your wounds are something I can't heal?

Who will I love when my heart is overflowing with compassion?

What do I do with these memories
Plastered on the walls of my heart?

Fresh

These wounds are still fresh
The sound of your kisses on my skin
Still echo through my senses
I still see you when I close my eyes
I hear you sleeping next to me
Until I realize I'm dreaming
Again
Remembering you
Again
I find my hands pressed against
My eyes and chest
It's the only places that replay you
Over and over
Day after day
These wounds are still fresh

Depletion

I slipped into the sea
Of my own thoughts
The day you neglected
To say you loved me
I found myself gasping
For the air you snatched away
Right from under my wings
I was an object to you
Prettier, more serene, more lovely
When my will would bend
And hail your ego
Like eb-n-flow
You drained the nutrients from my soul
Leaving pieces of me broken
Then whole
You infected me mentally
Until my every thought
Was keeping you happy
Just enough to keep me from breathing
I died the day you survived

Marla Mason

The Change Up

Disrespect became the dialect
Lovers turned into strangers
Who have we become
When the words we speak
Pierce hearts like daggers

Depression

Dark waters danced along the riverbed of my heart
I wanted to drown
Release the emptiness
Lonely
Wet
Spaces seeping through the old and worn crevices of my heart
I wanted a way out
I was tired of shouting
Crying
Singing
I wanted the silence to end

Have Me

How can I move on and love someone new?

You still have all the puzzle pieces of my heart

Your footprints are cemented
In the pathway to my soul

How can I move on?

You still
Have me

Confusion

I wish the confusion would end
Even if it means we must too.

Binge

Today I wish
I could lay in bed
Cry out these unsettling emotions
Binge on memories
Of anything and everything
Until this is released

Nostalgia

I remember singing
Softly into your heart
Watering the love
You harvested for me
I remember your air
It was soft and comforting
You were my safe place
My healing away from home
I remember loving you
Keeping you closer than anyone before
I remember nostalgia

You

You wrote the hieroglyphics of your love across my heart
Bound my soul with your words in sacred rituals
And left me in a world
That could never understand the inscriptions engraved in my being
No one to chant away your memories
You changed my life
In ways that left me desperate
For your touch
Because no one else understands
How to love me the way you do
And I wish it weren't you
I feel like I'll forever be bound
To you

My Day

I've fallen in love more times
Than I can count
Looked into the souls of men
Released earthquaking sighs
From the despair I've nurtured in my belly
I've danced on hot coals
Or was it eggshells that embrace these memories of lack
Where times' tables fold in half
I've been there
And back
And there again
Always counting down
Savoring the moments
We've spent
Reflecting on the time we have left
I've loved a thousand times
In a million different ways
Waiting for love
To see me
Waiting for my special day

Thoughts

I rant and rave about love
The complexity of my heart
Only because
I hope you'll read a piece
And think of me
Think of our love

Easy

I fall in love so easy no wonder
I'm here thinking
Trying to understand
Why love
Doesn't know my name by now

Cold

Take me to the place
You never abandon
I want to be there
With you
I cannot take the
Lonely corners of your heart
It's too cold there

Dark

I've lost my way to your heart
All the light has been consumed
By this darkness
Why haven't you come
Looking for me?
You were the only place
I'd called home
Who's love are you housing now?
How could you forget about
Our love?

Desperate

I've been desperate lately
Moving hastily
Forgetting to pray before my actions
Moving recklessly
Into tornado sized spirals
I think I've drained my heart of feeling
It's always bleeding
Left out to rot
As I chase these demons
I've been a fien
For her love
Or is it her attention?
I've made decisions
That haven't added up
Misfiguring figures, I've traded my own stock
Investments in myself
I traded for her love
How did I trade my value
For someone else's hopes and adoration?
Now I'm looking back
Wondering
Where to rest and hide from this devastation

Bleeding Heart

I felt pieces of you bleed
From the corners of my heart
It screamed out as if God made the pain
You gave me
How else could I endure your absence
I wanted you
Despite my illusions of love
I wanted to hold you
Again
I needed restoration
This loneliness is draining

Healing

Don't love me
I can't stop living to heal you
I don't have room for you to stay

Water

I waited for spring leaves to fall in autumn
You waited for my love in your season
The only problem is I cannot bloom
In dry soil
You never watered your heart
So why place me there?

Bloom

If I have to wait
I will
I've tried moving
These mountains
And my heart breaks
Every time I start digging
So I'll wait
Til this mountain between us
Has moved
And our love
Has a chance to bloom

Storybook

There is no need for an introduction
I've been here before
We've danced to this song
Carried this beat
In the belly of our souls
And lost the feeling
Like miscarried seeds
I wish I knew
How to accept
The love portrayed in storybooks
I wish I could wait
Find my love in my arms
Like a prediction of fate
But this is no fairytale
Yet, I'm the one
That keeps saving the princess
When will I find
My happy ending

DEAR GRIEF,

Your Pain Is Temporary

A Love Letter to Myself

Learn to control your emotions
Observe the tensions within yourself
Before calling out the defect in others
Acknowledge your mistakes and learn from them

Write
Cry
Write
Morn
Write
Release
Grow. Grow. Grow.

We all have cycles
In order to grow
We must overcome our shortcomings
And focus on growing
Evolving into your highest self

Modified

You shattered pieces of me
That were put together well
Pieces that I was proud of

Damaging words pierced my ears
In ways that left me deaf to positivity
Open to self humiliation
My esteem was annihilated

I was malleable and impressionable
You finally broke me

And soon after you reprogrammed who I was
Created your own image
You viewed yourself as a god
Wielding the minds of men
You turned myself against
Myself

I knew you were proud of what you'd accomplished
I could feel your enthusiasm

Every time you touched me
Every time you kissed me
I was yours

You used my gentle heart as a weak spot
My gentle hands to do your dirty work
My lips to consume your lies

I bent at the waist
To provide the submission you wanted
Stroked your ego the way you liked
All the while I was learning
To become strong enough to walk away
Strong enough to reprogram my mind

And rewrite my ending

Open

Why is it that I hide my heart with you?
I wish I could sing to you
I wish my insecurities didn't interfere
With my greatness but
Im human
With ideals
Too much of a dreamer
To live in reality
I wish I could lasso
The moon
Just to prove
I'd do anything
To share my heart with you

Changed Minds

I woke up
In the arms of my lover
Only to fall asleep
In the lap of despair

Growth Spurts

I wanted to grow old
With you
Except, I grew
And you became old news

Your Touch

Nights like this
Make me miss your touch
You held love there
Especially when
The world is so cold

Marla Mason

Impact

I fell in love with you
A thousand times
In a thousand different ways
I found myself in love with you
In ways I reserved for God
I wanted your love for reasons
That kept me breathing
Kept me striving to be better
I loved you timelessly
Over and over again
My heart beated for you
Even when your hands
Were hundreds of miles away
Loving you changed me

Good Mornings

I couldn't stop dreaming that night you were here
I was overstimulated
Your presence was oxygen
To my already burning flame
I saw you
The glow of your ora was magnificently
Bright
You touched my subconscious
Changed my views
I was in heaven after
Basking in your hues

Intoxicated

I want to drown in the rivers
Of your thoughts
Take me to the secret places
You hide your heart
Guide me through the depths of your soul
I want to lay there
And rest in your arms
Forgetting the world
That's left us wounded
Surround me with your presence
I just want to be with you

Hope

If I can write one word
A line
A poem
Daily
I can always begin my healing process
Always rebuild these shattered walls
In the fortress of my heart.

Happy

I watched my heart dance
The day I knew
I'd figured out the path
To you

Wife

Can you see me?

Beyond the words
I use to express pieces
Of me
Can you see me?

My whole frame
My body
Soul
My mind
And heart

Do you see the scars?
These beautifully deep memories
Of healed pain

Do you find yourself
Loving me?

All of me?

For as long as we share
The same air
Space and time?

Do you see me?

Your future wife

Energy

The words she spoke
Cleansed the deepest
Parts of my heart
Her voice chanted
Healing scripture
That nourished my soul
Her love cradled me
In the loneliest places
And even then
When her love covered me
Like blankets
I knew her energy
Matched mine
I knew I was the only one
She would call my everything

Best Friend

I need a delicate lover
One who takes their time
To learn the best pieces of me
I need a deliberate lover
Someone who loves
Without being asked
I need a calm lover
Someone to keep my thoughts inline
I need my lover
The one I've dreamt of since childhood
Someone who's my lover
And also my best friend

Marla Mason

Ocean

It seems these stages
Are flowing in and out
Of me
Like shorelines
And melodic notes
The old fades into the abyss
Regroups and creates something
New
Sometimes I want to start over
And forget the part
Where the waves crash
I want to be vast and steady
Like the heart of the ocean

DEAR HEARTBREAK,

It's Time For You To Forget My Name

Note To Self

When you clean house
Don't forget to collect the cobwebs
Between the door post where she left
And the door to your heart
When you clean house
Clean every inch

Freedom

I made peace with the demons he left
Learned their weaknesses and
Tamed them
Walked them
Taught them
Loved them
Then I released them
Turns out they
Weren't demons afterall
Turns out
They were the answer
To all the pain I carried
And built the walls
Of my heart on
Turns out
Setting them free
Allowed me to breath
And be who I've
Always been
Me
Without the influx of
Us

Delicate

My eyes danced with
Pleasure

The first time I saw your
Smile

I wanted to know your name
Now I know you were
Delicate

Not to be touched
You couldn't handle
The way I carry
My love

Im rough
At the Edges with
Sharp corners
My love cuts
Deep

There aren't any
Clouds to float off with
Just the slap of reality
No smiles just grind

You weren't ready
For my love
You should have
Stayed in
Your box Its
Safer there

Calling

I would call you because
I could feel your heart searching for me
Now I realize
It was your loneliness that screamed
Over the vibrations of your heart
We loved the empty spaces of each other
Never really making room for growth
Just for overnight visits
And late night soul searching
We fit each other in that way
We mirrored each others' steps
But our paths are different
It's no surprise, when you're gone
I can clean up in peace and get back
To creating my destiny

Slower

I feel the universe saying
Slow down
You're constantly growing
Learning
Processing
Understanding
You have to slow down
To apply these lessons
Love without boundaries
Be the best version of you
There's no need to rush

Yahweh

I prayed for change
Soaked in sacred oils
And released my consciousness
From society's ideals
I refrained from chemicals
Let my nails grow
My hair strengthen
The scales over my eyes deteriorated
My skin shed over and over until my true melanin was even
I began to glow
Like light bulbs in dark abandoned rooms
I felt every void filled with this light
No room for self doubt or hesitation
I finally began my work

Destination?

Simply a figment of social indoctrination

I prayed for change
Not knowing change was all in the power of my will
My ideals complicated the power I can easily willed
I prayed for me
It's no one's responsibility to empower Yahweh within me
Broken
Lost
Impressionable
Insecure
these are the ways society holds us near.

Pray for change.

Allow it to first emerge in you.
Pray for change
Yahweh is in you too.

Marla Mason

Hue

If only you knew
How your smile
Lights up a room
Maybe then you'd see
Everything in a brighter hue

Emerging

I find myself married to this pain
Holding onto your words like vows
Said at the altar
Embracing the insecurities
You wrapped in gifts of criticism
I find myself aborting the seeds
You dropped in my womb
Apologies for the misuse and abuse
Of my love
I kept finding myself faithful to your grief
like your failures are my own
And our success is dependent
On me
Lately,
I've found myself not giving a fuck
About your well being
Your needs
Your future
Lately,
I've been divorcing your notion
Of love
And romancing myself
Loving myself
Becoming the best version
You never thought I could be
These days I'm abundantly celebrating me

Marla Mason

Unbreakable

Stand taller
Than
The pain

Reflecting

If only you and I
Survived our lives
Than this journey to find you
Was worth
Every heartache
Every mistake
And lesson learned
If all this lead me to you
Then I've been doing life right

Time

Time passes through hourglass figures
Dance along romantic dance floors
I want to freeze frame our last touch
And escape in your arms again
Create butterfly kisses
In places reserved for love
Time may tell the story
We never planned to live
But our love makes those times bearable
Here's to doing time

In Deep

I remember the first time I laid my eyes on you
The moon shined over your glowing skin
And stained the silhouette of your being into the essence of my
memory

You were beautiful
Soft
Feminine

I smiled inside knowing that my dry jokes
Would never keep your interest
Despite my flaws I persisted
Because you were the catch of a lifetime
Since then I've been enthralled in the makings of you
From the way you walk
To the way you smile
You've got me

I want to dance through the timeline of your love
With you leading the way
Showing me things
I never saw in me
I want the good
The bad
The great
The ugly

I want to fall in love with you
Over and over again
Just like the first time my eyes
Realized beautiful was your tangible soul
I'm so happy you're in my life

Your Worth

Tell me the moments that take your breath away
I want to replay them in your world daily to make your soul smile
Tell me the things you miss most and
I'll make sure you never forget the moments when you made those memories
I want you to be happy
Beyond good mornings and I miss you
Beyond holding my tongue in heated arguments
I want you to sleep without worries and
Dream of your future without stress
I want you to dance and laugh and cry
Because you're happy
Blessed beyond belief
I want to create memories that leave you
Breathless blessed and loved
You deserve this and more
Never forget you're worth it all.

A Part

Just because we don't speak
Doesn't mean I don't write
About you
Our version of love
Your eyes your hands
Just because I don't tell you
I love you
Doesn't mean my heart erased your fingerprints
Or the recordings of your voice

It means you will always have a place
In my heart
Held in the timeline of my memory
Vested in the soil of my soul
It means those pieces we made together
Will be displayed in my museum of life
The chorus to my favorite song

It means I'm forever grateful
For the lessons you've taught me
Without loving you
There wouldn't be a better me
So, although we are no longer together
I still remember the good things

Have I

Have I told you about your smile lately?
How the moon whispered softly to me
Vomiting it's envy?
Have I told you how beautiful
You make everything around you?
It's as if your light saturates beyond my clouds
And into me
Feeding me
Hope
Love
Peace
Joy
Have I told you lately
That I'm falling for your heart?
That this is the first time
Since childhood
That my heart can breath
And smile all at once
Have I told you that your voice
Soothes me?
And my burdens disappear
It's as if God placed you here
Just in time to remind me
Just how good
Loving can be

All Me

When it all didn't make sense
You did
Bleeding out my thoughts
You cleared my vision
Refocused my steps
Aligned my intuition
You made me new
Where would I be
Without the birth of you

Miracle

Quiet the sounds of your mind
It can be chaos there
Lower the borders of your heart
There's healing there
Open the windows of your mind
Brilliance flows from there
You see
You're a miracle
Individually packaged
Slowly being unwrapped
The world has been waiting
For you
The genius amongst the stars

You're An Original

Never forget who you are
Never doubt your existence
You're here for a purpose
Your story is priceless

Rose

I've drifted into dark places
Where my mind needed recovery
Just like near drowning victims
I've danced with the demons
In my head
Until the reality of losing reality
Was too surreal for me
I've suffocated under the wave
Of emotions that rise in me
From time to time
I've cried
For reasons I don't want to talk about
I've sang to lift the pain
Of my day off my back
I've been through life
Once or twice
Ran
Cried
Kicked
Screamed
I've lived in the darkest places
Within myself
Yet im the rose
Budding through the
Concrete

In Love

Have I told you
How in love I've been feeling lately?
It's as if I can recall
This feeling
From thousands of years ago
It's as if
I'm finally walking into my own
Reclaiming who I've always been
I'm in love with life
And where I'm headed
This type of love
Is organic
Without pressure
Without expectations
Just pure bliss
I wish I could give this love
To everyone as a gift

Marla Mason

Self Love

I've fallen in love with you
I whispered to myself
She smiled and said to me
It's great to have you back
Oh how I've missed the way
You love me.

Fearless

I have the intuition of my mother
The kindness of my father
No wonder
I can hear the universe
When I close my eyes
No wonder
I love without regrets

Perfect

I've loved you
Before you were born
And the small curls on your head
Past your ears
I've loved you
In ways only my heart could stretch
I've loved you
Like the stars love the sky
Covering the darkest parts of the sea
I've loved you
Beyond the way I've imagined love
I've loved you
Because you've always loved me.
I know God is real
He sent you just for me

Dream

I had a dream the other night
You and your brother
Were holding hands
Walking through a wheat field
With orange groves and lavender
That stretched for miles
Your smiles were carefree
You played
And danced
And stood
Under an oak tree
I had a dream
That all my love
Were seeds
You
Your brother
The oak tree
The orange groves
The lavender and wheat fields
All were products of my love
Planted
Watered
Tilled
Nurtured
I had a dream
That I left you
Prosperity
Love
And health
That night
I dreamt in color

Marla Mason

Slipped

I've cried moons over you
Waiting for the day
I'd wake
And the tide
Carried my doubts
Away
I made room for you
Inside the land
I escaped to
Like a fetus in the womb
I serenaded you
I created you
Embedded your philosophy
In the strands of my thoughts
I weaved together our futures
And in these moments
You were my motivation
My being
My calling
Into existence
I remember birthing you
Like any mother to a child
You were thought of years
Before you came to life
I'm so happy you're here
Recreating you daily
With strokes of my mind

I cried moons over you

My gift

I'm so glad
That through life

You're the only thing
That hasn't slipped

Forgive Yourself

It's ok to forgive yourself
For believing in promises they never seemed to keep

It's ok to forgive yourself
For loving them
When it diminished your self worth

It's ok to forgive yourself
For the bad decisions
And for wanting them to stay

It's ok to forgive yourself
For the times you chose them
And not yourself

Every time you ignored your gut

Every time you gave them your heart
Before they knew how to carry you

It's ok to cry
And hear yourself say
I forgive you.

It is the most powerful step into and through your healing process

It is vital to your growth

It's ok to forgive yourself
And love yourself once more.

About the Author

Marla Mason is from Southern California. Growing up with two brothers in a well-rounded two parent household, Marla found peace while writing. Her freshman year in college was when she hit an emotional wall. It was caused by trauma that left her devastated. Without speaking about her internal scars, Marla wrote to heal herself. She opened up to her family about her truth and allowed her healing to be her writing. <u>When My Soul Was Undone</u>, is the product of that healing. Marla has written this poetry book in hopes that it will help someone else. Marla has two loving children and is currently living in Northern California, where she continues to write.

Made in the USA
San Bernardino, CA
08 July 2019